Contents

In order to protect the privacy of individuals featured in case studies, some names have been changed.

Words appearing in the text in bold, **like this**, are explained in the Glossary.

Are you in shape?

What sort of shape are you in? Do you ever feel tired or sluggish? Do you struggle to get motivated? Ask yourself if you'd like to be able to dance for longer, or not get out of breath doing small jobs. Do you want to feel great about your body?

The good news is that getting into shape doesn't have to be a drag. In fact, the best ways to get in shape are a lot of fun and you can get your friends involved, too. So whether you're skinny or large, sporty or a couch-potato, there is something in this book for you. Read on and find out how you can shape up and feel full of energy and confidence.

Getting into shape will boost your energy levels and improve your quality of life.

Ways to Get in
Shape

Charlotte Guillain

Raintree

www.raintreepublishers.co.uk
Visit our website to find out more information about Raintree books.

To order:
☎ Phone 0845 6044371
🖹 Fax +44 (0) 1865 312263
🖳 Email myorders@raintreepublishers.co.uk

Customers from outside the UK please telephone +44 1865 312262

Raintree is an imprint of Capstone Global Library Limited, a company incorporated in England and Wales having its registered office at 7 Pilgrim Street, London, EC4V 6LB – Registered company number: 6695582

Text © Capstone Global Library Limited 2011
First published in hardback in 2011
Paperback edition first published in 2012
The moral rights of the proprietor have been asserted.

Edited by Andrew Farrow and Vaarunika Dharmapala
Designed by Richard Parker
Picture research by Ruth Blair
Originated by Capstone Global Library Ltd
Printed and bound in China by South China Printing Company Ltd

ISBN 978 1 406 21747 6 (hardback)
15 14 13 12 11
10 9 8 7 6 5 4 3 2 1

ISBN 978 1 406 21775 9 (paperback)
16 15 14 13 12
10 9 8 7 6 5 4 3 2 1

British Library Cataloguing in Publication Data
Guillain, Charlotte.
101 ways to get in shape.
613.7-dc22
A full catalogue record for this book is available from the British Library.

Acknowledgments
We would like to thank the following for permission to reproduce photographs: Alamy p 25 (Leila Cutler); Corbis pp 6 (Rick Gayle Studio), 19 (Tom Stewart), 21 (Philip Harvey), 22 (Randy Faris), 23 (Darius Ramazani), 24 (Rolf Bruderer), 26 left (Image Source), 26 right (Shawn Frederick), 31 (Sean Justice), 36 (Michelle Pedone), 38 (Sam Diephuis), 42 (Brooke Fasani), 43 (Thomas Kruesselmann), 47 (Mango Productions); Getty Images pp 13 (Robyn Beck/AFP), 32 (Matthew Lewis), 45 (Andy Marlin/Stringer); iStockphoto pp 4 (Kristian Sekulic), 7 (Steve Debenport), 34 (omgimages), 37 (YanLev), 48 (Helder Almeida), 51 (PhotoTalk); Shutterstock pp 8 (Zaneta Baranowska), 10 (Gregory Gerber), 11 (Jason Stitt), 15 (Diego Cervo), 16 (Ariwasabi), 17 (HSBN), 27 (muzsy), 39 (Timothy Epp), 40 (Yuri Arcurs), 49 (Arpi), 50 (Yuri Arcurs).

Cover photograph of a mother and son carrying surfboards out of the water at a beach, reproduced with permission of Photolibrary (Blend Images/John Lund/Sam Diephuis).

Every effort has been made to contact copyright holders of material reproduced in this book. Any omissions will be rectified in subsequent printings if notice is given to the publisher.

Disclaimer
All the internet addresses (URLs) given in this book were valid at the time of going to press. However, due to the dynamic nature of the internet, some addresses may have changed, or sites may have changed or ceased to exist since publication. While the author and publisher regret any inconvenience this may cause readers, no responsibility for any such changes can be accepted by either the author or the publisher.

Quiz

How do you shape up?

1. It's the weekend. You plan to:
   - a. stay in bed as much as possible
   - b. go out skateboarding or dancing with your friends
   - c. go for a long run, followed by a swim, a bike ride, and a tennis match.

2. Your friend is over at your house. It's lunchtime and you are both hungry. You decide to:
   - a. get a takeaway
   - b. make sandwiches
   - c. go for a walk instead.

3. You've had a busy day at school and you've worked hard on your homework. You:
   - a. watch television in your bedroom
   - b. play computer games and chat with your family
   - c. go for a run.

4. What does a good breakfast mean to you?
   - a. doughnuts
   - b. fruit and wholemeal toast
   - c. nothing, you always skip breakfast.

Find out the truth!

If your answers were:

Mostly a's: there are many ways that you can become more active and have fun. Read this book to find some ways to get moving and take control of what you eat.

Mostly b's: you're in pretty good shape but you might still be surprised to learn some new ways to stay healthy in this book.

Mostly c's: you're an exercise fiend. That's great, but you need to take some breaks to relax, eat, and unwind. Read this book to find some new activities you might enjoy and other ways to stay relaxed and healthy.

You are what you eat

What you eat makes a big difference when you want to get in shape. A balanced diet is really important to keep us healthy and happy. But it's easy to get confused by all the information about food in magazines, on television, and on the internet. Read on to discover everything you need to know to make the right choices about food.

We all have to make some choices about what we eat. Would you rather have the apple or the muffin?

Here's some good news: popcorn is a healthy wholegrain! It's best to make it yourself or, if you buy it, make sure that it doesn't have too much added sugar or salt.

01 It's all about balance. Try to eat a range of different foods every day, including plenty of **wholegrains**, fruit, and vegetables. Try not to eat too many biscuits, crisps, cakes, or sweets.

What's that?

Wholegrains are the whole of the seed of a plant. If something is not wholegrain, parts of the seed have been removed, which means many vitamins and minerals have been lost.

02 Try to eat at least FIVE portions of fruit and vegetables a day. Fruit and vegetables are great in so many ways: they're full of **vitamins** and **minerals**, and they can help you maintain a healthy weight. They can also help to stop you getting diseases like cancer and heart disease.

03 Your body is growing fast, so it's no wonder you feel hungry all the time! Keep yourself going through your busy day with three regular meals. Choose foods that will fill you up. Wholegrains, fruit, and vegetables are great for this.

04 Set yourself a healthy food goal. Make it something simple and realistic but keep this goal in your head every day. It might be "I will eat fruit for a snack every day", or "I'll only eat crisps at the weekend".

05 Write your goal in your diary or put it on a notice board. Remind yourself what your goal is every day. Tell your family what your goal is and ask them to help you achieve it.

A healthy sandwich is great for filling you up and giving you energy.

Your five-a-day

You know you're supposed to eat five portions of fruit and veg a day, but do you actually do it? Here are some tips on how to get your five and feel alive!

06 Try and eat some fruit with your breakfast. You could slice a banana on to your toast or put some berries in your cereal. You could try eating an apple while you get ready for school. Then you're on your way to five before the day begins.

07 Drink your way to five! One glass of fruit juice or fruit smoothie counts as a portion. Just remember two or more glasses don't count as more than one portion.

08 If you want an easy snack on the move, try taking dried fruit to school with you. You could try dried raisins, apricots, apple, mango, pineapple, or figs. Check that they don't contain any added sugar.

09 If you're hungry before a meal, why not grab some raw vegetables, such as carrots, cucumber, celery, or tomatoes?

10 Sorry! Chips and roast potatoes don't count, even though potatoes are a vegetable. This is because they count as a **carbohydrate** instead. Baked potatoes are okay, though, and they are great for making you feel full. Try them with fillings such as bean chilli, tuna and sweetcorn, or cheese and tomato, to get another portion of veg into your day.

There are so many delicious fruits to choose from. Try as many varieties as you can and find your favourites.

Quiz

True or false?

a) dairy foods make you fat

b) vegetarians are healthier

c) a salad isn't always the healthiest choice

d) all breakfast cereals are good for you.

Find out the truth!

a: False. Some dairy foods such as cream, ice cream, butter, and cheese have a lot of fat in them. You should eat less of these or not eat them too often. But low fat yogurt and reduced fat milk and cheese are fine and you need them for **calcium** to make your bones strong.

b: False. Many vegetarians are healthy, but if they only eat cheese and chips then they're not! Everyone needs to eat a balance of different foods and avoid too much fat, sugar, and salt to be healthy, whether they eat meat or not.

c: True. In restaurants many salads come with dressings and extra toppings that are high in fat. Often a sandwich, a baked potato, or a pasta dish could be healthier. Try making your own salads.

d: False. Many breakfast cereals are high in sugar and salt and are not that different from eating a chocolate bar for breakfast! Try to choose wholegrain cereals that will fill you up and give you energy all morning.

11 Your body needs some **protein** every day so you can grow and stay healthy.

Here are some good ways to get protein into your day:

- have eggs or peanut butter on toast for breakfast
- eat a tuna fish or chicken sandwich for lunch
- if you are a vegetarian, beans and nuts are a good way to get protein.

12 You can get protein from **processed** meats like ham, sausages, and bacon, but watch how much you eat. These meats can have a lot of salt and fat in them and can be unhealthy if you eat them too often.

What's that?

When food is **processed** it has been prepared in a particular way, often using machines. Ingredients like fat, salt, and sugar may be added.

13 Want a quick dairy snack? A carton of fruit yogurt is a great way to get calcium and protein into your day. Just watch out for added sugar and look for low-fat choices.

Chicken is high in protein and low in fat, so it is a great addition to your diet.

Drinking plenty of water keeps your body **hydrated**. This helps you to stay focused and refreshed.

BE SMART

Think about your drinks!
What you drink is just as important as what you eat.

14 Try not to drink too many fizzy drinks. They can be full of sugar and that's bad news for teeth. Even diet drinks can damage your teeth. Save fizzy drinks for occasional treats.

15 Stay alert! You need to drink plenty of water or you might feel tired and run down. Try to drink six to eight glasses of water a day.

16 Your skin and hair look better when you drink enough water. Why not carry a reusable water bottle around with you and keep filling it up so you never run out?

17 Milk is another great drink. The calcium in it is good for strong teeth, bones, and fingernails. Breakfast is a good time to get your milk fix. You could add fruit to make a smoothie. Try to drink reduced-fat milk.

18 Juices like orange and cranberry are full of vitamin C. This helps your body to take in the **iron** you need. Look for labels that say "100% fruit juice with no added sugar".

"I drink lots of water which really helps to hydrate the skin and keep it looking fresh."

Poppy Delevigne, model

Is fat always bad for you?

No! Our bodies need some fats to help us take in vitamins and to give us energy. We also need fat under our skin to keep us warm and to protect us. Without fats in your diet your skin would look dry, your hair might fall out, and you could get ill more often.

What are the different types of fat?

There are two main types of fat – saturated and unsaturated. Saturated fat is in foods such as butter, processed meats, cream and ice cream, cakes, and biscuits. Too much saturated fat can lead to heart disease. Try to eat unsaturated fats instead, such as oily fish, avocado, nuts and seeds, and olive and vegetable oils.

19 If you're a big fan of cakes or chips, you don't need to cut them out of your life completely. Why not decide to have just a little once a week?

There is sugar in fruit, so is it bad for you?

This sugar isn't bad for you when you eat the whole fruit. But when we make fruit juice, the sugar is released and then it can be harmful. It's best not to drink too much fruit juice. Try to have it just at mealtimes. Drinking fruit juice while eating slows down the rate at which the body absorbs the sugar in it.

Can a veggie diet be balanced?

Lots of young people decide to become vegetarian for different reasons. But a veggie diet needs balance, too. It's important for vegetarians to think carefully about what they eat and make sure they're getting all the vitamins and minerals they need to stay healthy.

BE SMART

Veggie wisdom

Here are some tips for a balanced vegetarian diet:

- Plan the family's meals together so that there is always something for the vegetarian to eat.
- Get more involved with preparing meals and make your own packed lunch for school.
- Eat plenty of beans, nuts, eggs, and cheese to make sure you get enough protein.
- Eat plenty of wholegrains to get vitamins and minerals, and drink lots of milk to get calcium to make your bones strong.
- Green, leafy vegetables and dried fruit help to give you iron.
- You need to be careful not too eat too much food that is high in sugar, fat, and salt, just like everybody else!

Scott Jurek is a champion marathon runner. He is also a vegan, which means he eats no meat or dairy products.

Eat smart

Now we know all about eating a balanced diet. But how can we make the right choices if we don't know what's in the food we eat? How much should we eat and when should we be eating it? Is it wrong to snack? Read on for some top tips on how to find your way through the food maze and make the decisions that are right for you.

BE SMART

What is a portion?

Even if you're eating the right balance of foods, eating too much may make you put on unnecessary weight. Try to keep your portions to a healthy size.

- A daily portion of cheese should be about the size of three dominoes.
- Each portion of fruit and vegetables should be about the size of one of your handfuls. Remember, you're trying to eat five of these!
- The total amount of protein you eat every day should be about the size of a pack of playing cards.
- The starchy food in your meal, such as pasta, rice, or potatoes, should be about the size of your fist.

Looking at the labels on food packaging will help you to get control over what you eat. It may take a while to learn how to understand these labels but soon you'll need to only glance quickly at them to decide whether it's a "yes" or a "no".

listen up!

20 Look for food labels with the "traffic light" labelling system (see panel below). These labels make it easier to see what's in the food.

21 Most food labels will be a mixture of red, amber, and green. Try to choose food that has more green and amber and fewer reds.

22 If you're looking at food that doesn't have clear labelling then be careful! The food company might not want you to notice how much fat, sugar, or salt is in the food.

23 You can usually find ingredients on the back of food packaging. Which ingredients come first in the list? There will be more of these ingredients in the food than the ones lower down the list.

Traffic light labels

The traffic light labels on food packaging tell you how much fat, saturated fat, sugar, and salt there is in different foods. For example, if you see these colours next to salt you will know that:

- Red: the food is high in salt so it can be bad for your health if you eat too much. Only eat a small amount or don't eat this food very often.
- Amber: the food is not high or low in salt. It's okay to eat this most of the time.
- Green: the food is low in salt. The more green lights there are, the healthier the food is for you.

Get into the habit of checking the food labels on all the food you buy.

Q What does it mean if food is labelled "low fat"?

 A If a food is called "low fat" then it should have only 3 grams of fat in every 100 grams (0.01 ounces in every 3.5 ounces) of the food. But check whether this fat is saturated or not. It's also worth looking at how much sugar there is in it at the same time.

 Q What are calories?

 A Calories are a way of measuring energy. The calories on food labels tell us how much energy our body could get from the food. Our body uses up these calories when we grow and move. But if we take in too many calories we might put on weight. Exercise is a good way to burn up any extra calories.

Make sure the cereal bars you snack on don't contain too much sugar.

Snacks such as dried fruit and nuts release their energy slowly and keep you going for longer.

24 It's okay to have a healthy snack if you feel hungry. You're growing and your body needs fuel. Here are some ideas:

- a piece of fruit
- a slice of bread with peanut butter
- dried fruit and nuts
- a carton of low fat yogurt.

25 Watch the number of snacks you have in a day. If you're having more than two snacks as well as three meals then you're probably eating when your body doesn't really need more food.

26 If you're not sure how many snacks you have each day, try writing down everything that you eat. You may not realize how much food you eat that you don't really need.

27 Avoid snacking on sweets, chocolate, crisps, and biscuits. These are high in sugar and fat and won't fill you up or give you long-term energy. But they can make you put on weight.

28 Do you know when to stop eating? Listen to the signals your body sends you. If you feel uncomfortably full after a meal you have probably had too much. Try to eat less next time.

29 Do all your friends eat fast food? Is it hard not to join in? Try eating smaller amounts of this food less often.

You probably read a lot about how the latest celebrity diet can change your life. Do you think these diets really work? Or could they just be a way for people to make money selling books and products?

30 If you are really worried about your weight, go to your doctor. You should only go on a diet if you are sure your weight is unhealthy, NOT because you want to look like celebrities and models in magazines and on television.

31 "Crash diets" can make people lose a lot of weight very fast. But the rapid weight loss can be unhealthy, or made up of just water. When you start to eat normally again, you'll put all the weight back on and maybe more! It's better to eat healthily and exercise.

32 Stay away from "low carb" diets that tell you to keep off bread, pasta, rice, and potatoes. You need carbohydrates for energy. Instead, think about portion size and eat plenty of wholegrains, fruit, and vegetables.

33 Don't let your friends persuade you to try a diet. Try to be strong and remember what you know. They might lose a lot of weight to start with but if you want to have a healthy weight and keep it that way, you should stick to a balanced diet and get active.

34 Don't spend your money on diet shakes and snack bars. They are just a way for the manufacturers to make money. You're much better off making your own smoothies and eating some fruit or nuts.

case study

Don't diet!

Katy is a healthy weight for her age and height. But when her friends all went on a diet she decided to try it, too.

On this diet Katy could eat only two or three different foods. She didn't feel full after mealtimes but she drank lots of water to feel fuller. She lost quite a bit of weight in the first few days and her clothes felt looser. But she also felt dizzy, tired, and grouchy and her hair and skin looked bad. She couldn't concentrate at school and fell out with her best friend.

In the end, Katy gave in and ate loads of chips and ice cream. She put all the weight back on just as quickly as she'd lost it. She's decided to think about what she eats but not to worry about it. And she's doing more exercise because that makes her feel great. Now Katy looks much better than she did on the diet.

And the moral is ... Faddy diets don't work. They could make you feel terrible and if you do lose weight you will probably put it back on. Focus on being healthy and happy.

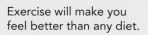

Exercise will make you feel better than any diet.

Quiz

True or false?

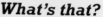
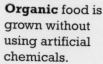

What's that?
Organic food is grown without using artificial chemicals.

a) eating a healthy diet can be boring

b) **organic** food is better for you than other food

c) cereal bars are always a healthy snack

d) a "low fat" or "light" food is better for you

e) you don't need to exercise if you eat less food.

Find out the truth!

a: False. With a balanced diet you can eat almost anything you like, as long as you eat more of the healthy foods and fewer of the foods that are high in fat, sugar, and salt.

b: False. Research has shown that organic food and non-organic food usually both contain the same **nutrients**. Some organic food can have more fat, salt, or sugar in it than similar non-organic food. Many people choose to eat organic food because of their beliefs, for example about the environment.

c: False. Many cereal bars have a lot of added sugar so always check the label.

d: False. When something is labelled "low fat" or "light" you're not getting the whole story. Always check the label to make sure the food isn't high in sugar or salt.

e: False. You may lose weight if you eat less food but if you don't exercise you will still be unhealthy. Exercise keeps your heart and lungs strong and tones up your muscles. If you are active then you will have a healthy appetite and there is no need to diet.

It's okay to eat some fast food but don't overdo it!

Are you wondering how to make a balanced diet part of your everyday life? Here are some ideas to help you stay in control:

35 Put the money you don't spend on fast food, chocolate, or crisps in a jar and save up for something you really want.

36 If it's hard to cut down on the amount of cheese you eat, try buying cheese that's lower in fat. Or you could buy a stronger cheese. You'll find you won't need so much of it.

37 Are your family buying too much of the wrong food? Talk to them about the problems some foods can cause. You could all try a new fruit or vegetable each week.

38 Get involved with the cooking at home. Try to use unsaturated vegetable oils instead of saturated fats like butter.

39 Lots of processed food that you buy in supermarkets is full of hidden fat, sugar, and salt. Find recipes to make your own homemade burgers, grilled chicken nuggets, and oven-baked chips.

40 Don't get stressed about food – enjoy it! Sharing a meal with friends is the best way to eat, so why not invite your mates over and experiment together with new foods?

Get active

Gone are the days when we had to go out with a spear and hunt for our dinner! We can drive to supermarkets and restaurants and our food is there, ready for us. We sit in school all day, and when we come home we can sit and play computer games or watch television.

Life is easy. But if you slouch around too much you can feel grouchy and uncomfortable and put on weight. It doesn't have to be that way! Just by making a few simple changes to your life you'll find that you can be much more active.

Moving around in the fresh air helps you to stay trim and toned and feel happier and more confident. If you make exercise a normal part of your day, it will also keep you healthy throughout your life. So what are you waiting for? Read on and get ready to MOVE!

Do these kids remind you of yourself?

The food you eat every day is your fuel. It helps you to grow and keeps all the parts of your body working. It also helps you to move around. If you don't move, this extra energy will stay in your body as fat. But the good news is you don't need to run a marathon or do 200 push-ups every morning. You can get your heart, lungs, and muscles to work harder while you go about your day.

41 Remember that goal you set to make your diet healthier? Now it's time to set a new goal to get more active. You might want to read this chapter first to get some ideas. When you've decided on your goal, write it down and remind yourself what you are trying to achieve every day.

42 People may have suggested that you walk to school. What's stopping you? If it's too far, try getting the bus some of the way and walk the rest. Walk with a friend and have a good chat before school. Walking gets your **circulation** moving and your heart working, so you'll arrive at school feeling full of energy.

43 If walking doesn't do it for you, can you ride a bike instead? You will get to places quicker than if you were walking. If the traffic is slow on a busy school morning you might even beat the bus!

Make exercise a part of your daily routine. You could walk to the places you need to go instead of taking a bus or getting a lift.

44 If you're feeling bored at home, go for a walk. You could go and see a friend or offer to fetch some shopping. Even if you just get out and walk in the fresh air for no reason, you will feel better.

45 If you find walking on your own boring, you could try listening to music on the way. The faster the music, the faster you will walk and the harder your heart and lungs will have to work! Just make sure you can hear the traffic and other people around you.

46 If it's hard to get motivated, try getting a **pedometer** to count the number of steps you take every day. You should be walking 10,000 steps. How close are you at the moment? You might be surprised! Once you start using a pedometer you'll want to walk more to reach your 10,000 target.

47 Try sitting on a yoga ball while you're at the computer or watching television. This will help improve your balance and coordination.

What's that?

A **pedometer** is a gadget that counts the steps you take in a day. It can motivate you to do more exercise. You can buy inexpensive pedometers in most sports shops.

If you listen to music when you walk, make sure you take care near traffic.

Oops!

Many young people prefer to play computer games or watch television after school rather than exercising. Some may get a lift to school so they can spend longer in bed in the mornings. But lying around can make young people feel uncomfortable and grumpy. They may put on weight and not have the energy to do anything about it. Other kids might tease them about being fat.

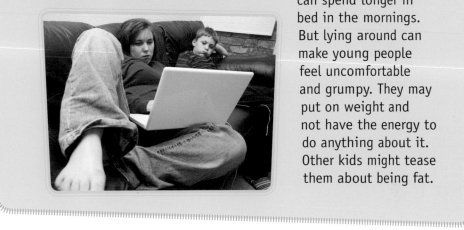

Get off that couch!

How can you make a change and get more exercise into your routine? Even the smallest changes make a difference and will help you to make other changes.

The great thing is, the more active you become the easier it is to keep going. So just take that first small step to feeling fitter. It won't take long before you feel and look better. You can still enjoy games and television but you won't be able to sit on the couch for too long without feeling restless!

BE SMART

Easy exercise
Here are some easy exercise ideas:

- Get up early so you have time to walk to school. You could listen to music on the way and when you get to school you'll feel more awake than usual.
- After school take the dog out for a walk or take your bike to the park.
- If you're bored, don't reach for a snack – get out for a walk.

48 It's often easier to get active with some friends. Why not take a frisbee to the park and see who wants to join in?

49 Join an after-school sports or swimming club. (You could use the money you would have spent on unhealthy snacks or computer games to join!)

50 Take a kite out on a windy day. This is great for your hand-eye coordination. Your reactions will get faster and you might get good at some unusual stunts.

51 Practise football, basketball, or netball with a friend.

BE SMART

Boredom busters
Here are some other things you could try if you are bored:

- Dust off your rollerblades or skateboard and get outside. You'll quickly get better at skating. Are there any skate parks near where you live?
- Find a rope and do some skipping.
- If you have a garden, help out with digging and weeding.
- Wash the family car.
- Go for a bike ride with family or friends.

Skipping isn't just for little kids! Boxers train by skipping because they know it strengthens their muscles.

Q I've always been really skinny so I don't need to exercise, do I?

A Exercise isn't just about losing weight. We should all be active, whatever body shape we have. Activity keeps our heart and lungs healthy and makes our bones and muscles stronger. It also makes most people feel more energetic, happier, and more confident. It also helps them to sleep better, too.

Q Games like table tennis and bowling aren't really exercise, are they?

A Table tennis is an Olympic sport! Matches can last for hours and the players have to run around a lot. Bowling gets you active because you are moving around and stretching. It's even better if you can walk to the place where you play these games!

You might be surprised at how tiring table tennis can be!

Oops!

It's easy to make choices that stop you getting active. We can be very good at making excuses! Here are some common traps that can stop you moving:

52 You get in from school. You're tired and you just can't wait to play your latest video game. Stop! Before you hit the games why not get out for a quick walk or run in the fresh air? This will help you shake off the day and you'll be much more alert when you start playing. Watch your new scores rack up!

53 It's the weekend. You roll out of bed and have the whole day ahead of you. You reach for the television remote. Stop! The television will be there later. Get out on your bike or skates and see if your friends are around.

54 You're all set to go out but it starts raining. You decide you are not walking in this weather. Stop! You could dig out an umbrella or put on a waterproof and just go out anyway. So what if you get wet? You can always get changed when you get back home!

55 You're all set to walk to school but your friend drives past in his parents' car and offers you a lift. Stop! Do you really want to spend the morning sitting in traffic? Why not see if your friend wants to join you walking? It would be a chance to chat without his parents eavesdropping!

Just remind yourself that you actually have fun and feel loads better when you get out and move!

Transfer your skills

If you play lots of computer games your hand-to-eye coordination is probably very good. This will help you to play sports such as ball games.

I'm overweight and I'm worried people will laugh at me when I exercise. What should I do?

You don't have to put on a leotard or jump over hurdles to exercise. Nobody will laugh at you for walking. Try to walk a little bit further and faster every day. If you get a pedometer (see page 24) you will feel really motivated as you see how much progress you make.

I don't know how to ride a bike. Is it too late to learn?

It's never too late to learn! It's easiest to learn on a bike that is slightly small for you. Make sure you can put your feet flat on the ground with your knees bent. Then find a quiet place and practise freewheeling along and try to keep your balance. Don't even try to use the pedals until you can scoot along and balance properly. Good luck!

"As long as I'm eating right, exercising, and being the best I can be, I will celebrate the person I am today!"

Tyra Banks, television star

"I don't DO sports!"

Are you one of those people who don't "do" sports? What's putting you off? Maybe you hate going outside in cold weather? Do you feel embarrassed playing in a team when you're not very good at the game? Or perhaps you're afraid that others will laugh at you because you're a bit overweight?

But if you don't do any exercise you might put on extra weight. Furthermore, research shows that young people who don't exercise are more likely to be depressed or stressed. So what's the answer?

listen up!

Here are some reasons why we should all get moving:

- **aerobic** exercise helps to stop heart disease, cancer, and **diabetes**
- **weight-bearing** exercises help to build up strong bones that don't break easily
- getting active tones up your muscles and gives you a firmer body shape
- doing some exercise in the fresh air can make you feel more positive, confident, and relaxed
- if you are genuinely overweight, exercise will help you to lose any extra pounds by burning off the excess fat on your body.

"I've never liked sports – I could never run as fast as the other kids and I always get picked last for teams at school."

Ayesha, 14

> "I've never been any good at sports. I'm useless at football, and I can't catch a ball. I like watching sports, especially tennis and athletics, but I've given up trying myself."
>
> Sam, 15

The key to getting energized is to find a form of exercise that fits in with your life. Try to combine some aerobic activity with exercise that makes you flexible and tones your muscles, such as yoga. Just remember the golden rule: the longer you do something, the better you get at it. So don't give up!

case study

Marathon man!

Adam's dad, Jonathan, was overweight when he was at school. He didn't exercise because he wasn't in any sports teams. When he left school, he was unhappy with the way he felt and looked. Then he started running and cycling. Gradually he got stronger and fitter. Jonathan has just run his 32nd marathon and cycles 30 kilometres (20 miles) to work every day! Here is his advice:

> *"Exercise is for everyone. Your health is more important than anything. Who cares what other kids are doing – you need to focus on getting yourself fit and healthy. Set yourself small goals to start with and find a sport that suits you. If you like watching tennis then you already know the rules and you'll feel motivated to learn the game. Just remember, having fun and getting fit is more important than winning or getting into teams. Just get out there and go for it!"*

You can find a way to exercise that suits you.

Step up a gear

So you've changed your lifestyle to get more activity into your day. The next step could be to get into some organized activity. There are so many upsides to playing sports and trying active hobbies. You'll meet new friends and get more confidence from trying new things.

The good news is that there's something for everyone. If you hate football, or dancing makes you dizzy, don't worry! You don't have to do something just because your friends like it. There'll always be something else you can try.

If you are disabled, there are organizations that can provide the equipment you need to give just about any sport a try. The charity Get Kids Going! has helped many young disabled people to compete in sports at the highest level, including the Paralympics.

> **"My advice to any young disabled person is simple – get out there and try a sport."**
>
> Adam Field, wheelchair tennis player

Adam Field first started playing sports at school. He has gone on to represent the United Kingdom at international tennis tournaments.

Quiz

What sport best suits your personality?

1. It's the summer holiday and you have no plans. Would you like to:
   a. Get a group of friends together with a ball?
   b. Head to the pool or beach?
   c. Sit on your own in the shade with a good book?

2. You have to make a speech to your whole school. How does this make you feel?
   a. It will be okay if your friends are there
   b. No problem
   c. Oh no! What will you wear? Who will be watching? Do you have to do it?

3. Your school is having a sports day. How do you feel about this?
   a. It's okay, you'll all have fun together
   b. Great, you can't wait!
   c. Terrible. You hate performing in front of other people.

Find out the truth!

If your answers were:

Mostly a's: you are happy hanging out with other people and a team sport might suit you best. Look for a club where you can play with people at your level.

Mostly b's: you are quite confident and may already enjoy sports and activities. Why not try something new or different that will really interest you?

Mostly c's: you're not keen on the idea of sports, are you! It might suit you to try an activity that you can do on your own or with a close friend so you can slowly get more confident. If you set yourself small goals you'll probably get really focused quite quickly.

33

Think outside the box

56 Why not set yourself a goal to try a new activity? Be realistic and choose something that you can easily fit into your routine.

57 With so many different types of dance, there's something to suit everyone. You might want to learn some hip-hop moves, or learn Latin, or ballroom. Jive and tap will burn off a lot of energy. Choose what suits you best and find a class nearby.

58 Here are some ideas for team sports you could try:

- Football is easy to play – you just need a ball and some friends!
- Basketball or netball are games you can play with a group of friends and a ball. You could also join a team and play matches. If you can put up a hoop outside your house or use a public court to practise shooting, then you will soon get better.
- If you want to learn how to play rugby, it's best to join a club. It's a **contact sport**, which means you could get hurt without a coach to teach you properly.
- Find out if your local cricket club coaches players your age. They should be able to lend you all the equipment you need.

What's that?

When we play **contact sports** such as rugby, ice hockey, or martial arts, we come into physical contact with other people. It's important to know the rules to avoid getting hurt.

Try playing volleyball with a group of friends.

> **"Talent wins games, but teamwork and intelligence wins championships."**
>
> Sam, 15

Q Why should I warm up before I exercise?

A You are more likely to injure your muscles if they're not warmed up. Do some gentle activity that makes your heart beat faster and moves the muscles you will be using. If you are about to go jogging, then it's best to warm up for five minutes first by walking briskly or skipping. Talk to your sports teacher to get some good ideas.

Q Why do I need to stretch after I exercise?

A Again, you are less likely to get an injury and it will stop your muscles feeling sore later. It's a good idea to stretch your muscles while they are still warm after exercise. Your coach or PE teacher will be able to show you some good stretches.

Q How long and how often should I exercise?

A Try to do an exercise that makes you feel slightly out of breath for 60 minutes each day. You don't have to do it all at once!

Going it alone

Team sports are not for everyone. If you want to go it alone there are plenty of activities you can do. If you are exercising alone, tell someone where you will be and make sure you feel safe and comfortable there.

59 Get running! You'll just need some good running shoes and a watch. Start by running for five minutes, then walking for five minutes. Keep this up for 20 minutes. (See page 37 for more running tips.)

60 Have you tried other athletics? If you're tall, you might be good at long jump or high jump. If you're strong, you could try throwing the javelin or discus. Visit your local athletics club to see what activities are available.

61 Swimming is a great sport for burning off extra calories and getting your heart beating. It can be relaxing to swim up and down the pool at your own pace. Try swimming faster or further each time you go swimming to see how you've improved.

62 Activity in water is also great if you are disabled or recovering from an injury. Swimming is good if your doctor advises against a weight-bearing or high-impact exercise.

Swimming is great exercise for your whole body.

Run a little every day and you'll soon see a big improvement in your fitness levels.

case study

Love to run

Casey and Dani had never been into sport, and they were both getting a bit overweight. But they didn't know what to do about it. Then Casey's aunt started to train for a fun run. She persuaded the girls to go out on a training run with her and they caught the bug!

Casey: "I thought it would be too hard because I've never been able to run far. But we started off just running for five minutes and then walking for five minutes. We were still able to chat the whole time. After a while we started to run more and walk less until we could run for the full 20 minutes."

Dani: "We felt really motivated because every time we went for a run we could see we were going further. We wrote it all down in a notebook so we could see what we'd achieved. We feel really proud of ourselves!"

Now Casey and Dani feel much fitter and their muscles are more toned. Running is free and they can go at a time that works for them. They love being able to exercise together because there is always something to talk about!

And the moral is ... Anyone can run. The hardest part is getting yourself out of the door! Once you see how quickly you can get better at running you won't want to stop.

63 Activities such as yoga and pilates work on your strength and balance. These exercises can improve your posture and your body shape, and make you feel more confident.

64 If you can get out into the countryside then hiking is a great way to exercise. If you plan to go a long way, it's best to go in a group with an adult. Remember to take plenty of water.

65 If you are disabled, cycling can be a great activity. There are fantastic bikes available for all types of disability and if you join a club you may not have to buy your own equipment.

66 Martial arts are another good way to improve your balance and coordination. They can also help with your confidence and concentration. You could try:

- karate
- judo
- tae kwon do
- jujitsu
- kung fu

Learning a martial art can really boost your confidence.

67 You don't have to live near a mountain to go rock climbing. Find a centre near you with a climbing wall. An instructor will show you how to use the equipment. If you like it, then a climbing club might be a good way to try climbing in the great outdoors!

68 Try tennis, squash, or badminton if you are competitive. Most sports centres will hire out rackets when you book a court so try out the game before you spend any money on expensive equipment.

69 Gymnastics is a good activity if you want to build strength and flexibility and improve your balance. You can also try the trampoline. You'll start to feel more confident as your body shows you what it can do!

If you have a GPS device you could try **geocaching**.

"No one is born being good at things – you become good at things through hard work. You're not a varsity (university team) athlete the first time you play a new sport."

Barack Obama, President of the United States

The actor Jake Gyllenhaal likes to relax by skateboarding around New York City. Justin Timberlake and Jessica Biel prefer a spot of snowboarding. Barack Obama likes bodysurfing in Hawaii. Why don't you try something a bit different, too?

listen up!

70 If you're lucky enough to live by the sea, then get in the water. You could start off with bodysurfing, which is riding the wave without a board. When you're happy with that, try hiring a bodyboard or surfboard. You could take lessons to get you started, or to learn some tricks.

71 Do you live near a lake or river? Perhaps you could try kayaking? You need to be able to swim. Join a class and you will be provided with the equipment.

72 If you can get to the slopes, why not give snowboarding a go? You can also try it at indoor ski centres. It's great for building strong leg muscles and **core strength**.

What's that?

Core strength is built by working the muscles in your back and abdomen. These muscles keep your whole body stable and balanced.

Surfing is a great form of exercise. It is good for muscle tone, increased energy, and core strength.

Water sports

Windsurfing will strengthen the muscles in your arms and legs and tone you up. If you want to try something even more daring, take a look at kitesurfing. A kite pulls your board through the water. You need equipment and lessons though, so it could be expensive.

Oops!

It's easy to undo all the work you've done to get in shape by making a few unhealthy choices. Here are some tips to help you stay in shape AND in control:

73 You may be offered alcohol as a way to relax and have fun. If you want to stay in shape, turn it down! Alcohol can damage your growing brain, liver, and heart. It can make you take risks that could be dangerous for your health. Alcohol even makes you put on weight.

74 People start smoking for many different reasons. Some want to look cool, and others think it will stop them eating too much. If you want to stay in shape, don't smoke. It could give you cancer, heart disease, and other health problems. Smokers find it difficult to take exercise because they get out of breath quickly. It's hard to give up once you've started and it's very expensive.

75 Illegal drugs are substances that change the way people's bodies work. You may be offered drugs as a way to have fun. If you want to stay healthy, walk away. You don't know what drugs can do to your developing brain and the rest of your body. They might also make you take risks that could damage your health.

Keep it real

Do you ever think you will never look right? Do you compare the way you look to your friends? Do you look at celebrities in magazines and on television and feel you can never achieve their "perfect" look?

Many young people feel unhappy about the way their body looks, even if they are fit and healthy. But the reality is, we come in all different shapes and sizes and that's just fine. Think about what you value most in your friends. Perhaps they are funny, clever, or kind? These are the things you should look for and value in yourself. Read on, get wise, and learn to love yourself!

Each of us is unique and
that's the way it should be!

Don't be negative. Focus on what you like about the way you look.

76 Stick with your exercise. You will feel strong and healthy and your self-confidence will grow.

77 What goes around comes around. Tell your family and friends how good they look. Not only will this make them feel great but they're more likely to say good things about you, too.

78 Talk to your family and friends about what you see in music videos and in magazines. Why do pictures of models make so many people feel unhappy about their bodies? Do you think these models are happy and healthy?

79 Remember that your body is changing. It will become very different as you grow and develop. Give yourself a break! If you are eating a balanced diet and staying active then your body is just fine.

80 Every evening, think of three things that you did well or that made you happy during the day. Focus on positive things about yourself and try to ignore any negative thoughts. You could write your positive thoughts down and look back at them if you ever feel unhappy.

"I had been on this insane diet for almost 17 years to maintain the weight that was demanded of me when I was modelling. My diet was really starvation."

Carré Otis, model

81 Remind yourself that being in shape does not equal being thin. Write this down and put it on your notice board! Healthy bodies come in all shapes and sizes. Being in shape does not mean a certain body type.

82 Don't be fooled by photographs of models and celebrities in magazines. Many of these photographs have been changed to make people look thinner, remove spots, or make their hair look shiny. You're not a photograph – you're real! Don't even try to live up to these fake images.

83 Are you teased about the way you look? Stay calm and don't let it get to you. Remind yourself that often people tease and bully others because they are unhappy themselves. Tell a parent or teacher if you are teased a lot.

84 If you know someone who is unhappy with their body and not eating properly, talk to them. They need to know you care. Talk to a trusted adult if you are very worried.

85 If you feel unhappy about your body a lot of the time, talk to a parent, teacher, or your doctor. Tell them what you are worried about. They will reassure you and give you some practical suggestions to make changes if you need to.

Airbrushing
Changing photographs to make the people in them look "perfect" is called airbrushing. Some people think that all airbrushed photos should be labelled so that we know they are not completely real. What do you think?

Celebrity body troubles

Many models and celebrities feel they have to live up to an unrealistic idea of what a perfect body is. They are under so much pressure to look good that many have **eating disorders**. But celebrities are fighting back.

The singer Kelly Clarkson began to worry about her body when she was at school. She lost a lot of weight, but when her friend told her he was worried about her, she got a grip. Now she says, "I've got a butt … I can't help that. And I think it's good for people to see normal." Kelly's attitude proves that self-confidence, hard work, and enthusiasm are much more important than being skinny.

The model Kate Dillon suffered from **anorexia** for seven years. She was very thin but was still told to lose more weight! Then she gave up modelling and focused on getting healthy. Now she works as a "plus-size" model and is happy with the way she looks. She says, "I love my body … I've done better as a "big" girl than most "skinny" girls do as skinny models, so it's been amazing. But what's more amazing is that I did it on my own terms."

And the moral is … We are all different. It's more important to be happy with yourself than try to be what you think other people want.

Kate Dillon is much happier now that she is a normal and healthy size.

Q We keep hearing how unhealthy it is to be **obese**. So, what's wrong with wanting to be thin?

A Obesity is a dangerous problem. Carrying too much extra body weight can lead to diseases like cancer, heart disease, and diabetes. But becoming too thin can be equally dangerous. Eating too little deprives your body of the vitamins and minerals it needs. Try to maintain a healthy weight for your height by eating a balanced diet and staying active.

Sometimes it can be tempting to over-exercise as a way to lose weight. Here are some tips on keeping your exercise in check:

listen up!

86 Keep a record of when you exercise and how long each session lasts. Make sure you are building in days when you take a break. If you exercise for too long and too often you could get injured. Your muscles and joints need time to rest if you want them to work well.

87 Do you spend a lot of time thinking about your next exercise session or class? Do you exercise more than once a day? Do you feel stressed if you miss a day's exercise? You may be over-exercising. Talk to your doctor or sports coach and work out a healthy programme of activity for you.

88 Try to do more than one activity. It's much healthier to exercise in a range of ways so parts of your body get to rest. It's also good to exercise with other people some of the time, not just on your own.

89 Get some other hobbies. If all your free time is spent doing sport then it can be easy to get obsessed. Find some other activities you enjoy to help you relax and socialise.

90 Try not to see sport as a way to get a "perfect" body. That's not the point of exercise. Do it to feel fit, have fun with friends, and love your *healthy* body.

Q What is anorexia?

A Anorexia nervosa is a dangerous eating disorder and a mental health condition. People with anorexia are very worried about being overweight and are desperate to be thin. Often they will eat very little or nothing at all to become thin. Even if they are already far too thin and underweight, they continue to want to lose weight.

Q What is **binge** eating?

A Binge eating is when someone eats a lot of food until they feel sick. They often eat to feel better or because they are stressed, but they feel very unhappy after bingeing.

Q What is **bulimia**?

A Bulimia is an eating disorder where people binge on food, but then make themselves sick so they do not put on weight. It is a condition that can lead to very dangerous health problems such as damage to the heart, kidneys, and bowel. It can also cause tooth decay.

Doing too much of anything, including exercise, is bad for you.

Healthy body, healthy mind

Phew! There is so much to think about when we look at food and fitness. Sometimes it can feel overwhelming. Your life is busy enough with school, homework, and keeping up with friends. Not to mention getting on with your family!

Does your busy life ever make you feel stressed? Maybe you feel under pressure to do well at school and fit in with your friends? You're not alone if sometimes it all feels too much. But the good news is there are lots of ways you can take control and give stress the boot. Here are some tips on how to keep your mind as healthy as your body. Here are some ways to stay positive about yourself:

You may have a lot on your mind, but try not to feel stressed. It will only make things worse.

> **"No one can make you feel inferior without your consent."**
>
> Eleanor Roosevelt, wife of former US President Theodore Roosevelt

91 Don't expect too much of yourself. Set yourself small goals. For example, if you want to get fitter, make small changes to begin with, such as walking to school three days a week. You can set new goals later, and you'll feel good seeing how much you've achieved.

92 It's all about you. Don't waste your time trying to do what you think your friends want. Think about what *you* really want. You'll feel much happier making changes for yourself and doing what you really enjoy.

93 We all make mistakes! Don't get hung up on things that have gone wrong for you. The great thing about mistakes is that we can learn from them. Just think about how you could do things differently next time and then move on.

94 Don't waste time with people who make you feel bad about yourself. Real friends make you feel happy about who you are. You can tell your friends something you think is great about them, too.

95 If something is worrying you and the problem won't go away, don't try to ignore it. Talk to someone you trust and you'll feel better straight away.

Having a laugh with friends is always a good way to feel better.

Stress-busting

We all need to take time out from our busy lives and just chill. Here are some top tips on ways to relax and bust the stress:

96 Keep talking. You always feel better when you talk to your friends or family. You might keep in touch through networking sites or by texting. But nothing beats a good old fashioned face-to-face chat!

97 Curl up with a good book and lose yourself in a story.

98 A walk in the fresh air is a great way to beat stress. You often have time to think problems through and may come back with a solution. Walking with someone else is also a great way to talk about anything that is worrying you.

99 Forget about your worries and play your favourite computer games. But beware! Some games can get the **adrenalin** pumping and could make you feel more stressed than when you started!

100 Remember the simple things? Do some drawing or painting, ride your bike, or take a warm bath. All these things could make you feel surprisingly relaxed.

Activities such as yoga are great for stress-busting.

101 Sit somewhere quiet, close your eyes, and breathe deeply. Think of a place or person that makes you feel happy, and focus on that image in your mind. Try to do this for five minutes every day.

So now you're ready to take control of your life! Why not pass this book on to a friend?

Sort out what you eat and how you exercise and your body and mind will both be healthier.

listen up!

Remember, only one person can make you fit and healthy, and that's you. Perhaps you only need to make a few changes, or you know you need a completely different lifestyle. Whatever your situation is, don't be hard on yourself. Eating well and staying active are the two best ways to feel happy, so try and enjoy yourself while improving your life.

Just take things one step at a time and see what you can achieve. Always try to have a new goal to aim for, and don't forget – you don't have to cut out treats altogether! You can enjoy any food you like, as long as you get the balance right.

Glossary

adrenalin hormone that increases the heart rate as well as feelings of stress or panic

aerobic type of activity that uses arm and leg muscles and makes the heart and lungs work hard

anorexia eating disorder that causes sufferers to avoid eating because of a fear of weight gain

binge eat or drink too much

bulimia eating disorder where sufferers overeat and then vomit, over-exercise, or starve themselves

calcium mineral that strengthens teeth and bones

carbohydrate type of nutrient we get from food. The body breaks carbohydrates down into sugars that it uses for energy.

circulation movement of blood around the body, supplying energy and oxygen to all body parts

contact sport sport where players are likely to come into contact with each other. Contact sports can be very rough.

core strength strength of muscles close to the spine that help with stability

diabetes condition where the body is unable to process sugar properly

eating disorder condition where someone has unhealthy attitudes and behaviours related to food and weight

geocaching outdoor activity using a GPS device to find a specific location

hydrate absorb water

iron mineral we need to help carry oxygen around our bodies and to make many parts of our bodies work properly

mineral substance that comes from non-living sources, such as the rocks that break down and become part of the soil. Our bodies need minerals to work properly.

nutrient substance found in food that is essential for life

obese very overweight so that it is unhealthy

organic food grown without using artificial chemicals

pedometer gadget that counts the steps you take in a day. It can motivate you to do more exercise.

processed food that has been prepared in a particular way, often using machines. Ingredients such as fat, salt, and sugar may be added.

protein nutrient that provides the raw materials the body needs to grow and repair itself

vitamin nutrient that the human body needs to grow and stay healthy

weight-bearing type of exercise that strengthens bones. Weight-bearing exercises force muscles to push against something. They include jogging, aerobics, and dancing.

wholegrains whole grain seed of a plant, containing vitamins and minerals

Find out more

Books

Body Needs: Carbohydrates for a Healthy Body, Hazel King (Heinemann Library, 2009)

Do It Yourself: Keeping Fit – Body Systems, Carol Ballard (Heinemann Library, 2008)

Eat Smart: A Balanced Diet, Louise Spilsbury (Heinemann Library, 2010)

Health Zone: Stay Fit! How You Can Get in Shape, Matt Doeden (Lerner, 2008)

Websites

www.5aday.nhs.uk
A website with lots of tips on how to get more fruit and veg into your diet.

www.eatwell.gov.uk/agesandstages/teens
The Food Standards Agency's "Eat Well, Be Well" website is full of information to help you make healthy choices about your diet.

www.eatwell.gov.uk/foodlabels/trafficlights
Another section of the Food Standards Agency's website explains about "traffic light" food labels.

www.nhs.uk/Change4life
This website will help you set yourself small goals to change your lifestyle and become healthier.

www.yheart.net
The British Heart Foundation has lots of information on healthy lifestyles.

www.youngminds.org.uk/young-people
Visit this website if you need help with stress, anxiety, or any other mental health problems.

Useful organizations

Get in touch with these organizations to help you stick to your goals and stay in shape.

Bikeability
www.bikeability.org.uk
This organization teaches young people the skills they need to cycle safely. If you go on one of their courses, you will feel more confident to get out and use your bike more often. Visit their website to find out about a course near you.

Scouts
www.scouts.org.uk
The Scouts is a great organization for getting involved in physical outdoor activities. Visit their website for more information.

Urban Cricket
www.ecb.co.uk/development/kids/urban-cricket
This organization provides facilities in cities such as London, Birmingham, Newcastle, and Cardiff so that young people can play cricket whenever they want to. Visit their website for more details.

Topics to research

- What do you think about organic food? Find out more about the reasons why some people choose to grow and eat organic food. Do you agree with them?

- Take a look at the labels on some best-selling breakfast cereals that are targeting young children. Which ones have the most sugar and salt in them? Are there any cereals aimed at kids that aren't high in sugar and salt?

- Why do you think people buy bottled water? What are the problems with bottled water? What are the alternatives?

Index